By Jay Pierso....

Dedication

Many thanks to Krause Publications and John Gunnell, Mary Sieber,
Bob Hall, Ron Kowalke, Brad Bowling and, especially, to the kind readers
of *OLD CARS* weekly.

Published by

**krause
publications**

700 E. State Street • Iola, WI 54990-0001
Telephone: 715/445-2214

Library of Congress Catalog Number: 93-80698
ISBN: 0-87341-296-6
Printed in the United States of America

Introduction

Jay Leno and Jay Piersanti have some things in common. Both collect cars and both are full-of-fun funny men. Leno tells jokes on television's "Tonight Show," while Piersanti draws *Old Cars* newspaper's "Otto Mechanic" cartoon.

Otto and his gang have been around for more than a decade bringing laughs and smiles to the faces of old car enthusiasts every week. This book brings you classic cartoons from the early days of this popular comic strip.

Inside these pages, you'll find Piersanti at his comic and artistic best, using his id and his inkwell to remind all of us that the old car hobby is supposed to be a bunch of fun. His clean-cut (G-rated, of course) sense of humor is suitable for the entire family, yet very, very funny. Otto and his friends will have mom, dad, and the kids "rolling in the aisles."

The comic characters you'll meet include rascally Reo, Overland the mailman, the ever-lovable VIN and Otto's "significant other" named Polly. This family of funny folks will lighten your spirits and make you chuckle again and again.

"Otto Mechanic" is what old car collecting is all about ... happiness, high spirits, and humor ... all mixed in with a large dose of good, clean family fun.

La-da-dee-da-dee-da ... be happy! Read "Otto."

The Jay Piersanti Story

Old Cars cartoonist Jay Piersanti was born in Hamburg, New York in 1951 and still lives there. He tells us that Hamburg is a suburb of Buffalo, except in the winter when it disappears under the snow for three months. Jay's first memory is playing with the radio antenna control knob on his father's 1951 Buick Super.

Jay first got into cars through speed feats. He claims that his first auto racing experience was "my brother and I rolling around in the back seat of the ol' man's 1955 Century, as he challenged the rear tires to remain in contact with the asphalt at every intersection and stoplight." He also rode shotgun when his brother "blew off" a new 1963 Corvette by holding their father's 1959 Invicta in low gear up to 75 miles per hour. "Needless to say, the Twin Turbine Dynaflow was never the same after that," Piersanti recalls now. "My mother later concluded that she caused the damage by getting stuck in the snow."

In 1967, Jay made an unscheduled pit stop when the engine fell out of his 1964 Corvair while he was on a heavy date with Barbara, his bride-to-be. The bottom did not fall out when they married in 1976.

Piersanti entered the automotive art world, in 1968, by drawing the Chevrolet crossed-flags emblem during a study hall. He loved that race-bred badge that graced so many fenders of vehicles in his favorite magazine, *Car Craft*. Jay even considered adding big-block SS 396 emblems to his 1965 Impala SS, which actually had a small-block 283-cubic-inch V-8.

A significant educational experience occurred in 1969 when a student named Keith, in the next dorm room at Cornell University, turned out to be a "motorhead" with a 1957 Studebaker Golden Hawk and a 1964 Dodge 440. "I learned more from him than from all of my professors," Piersanti explains. "But, probably because I didn't go to classes too often."

In 1974, Jay took delivery of a 1974 Camaro with a 350-cubic-inch four-barrel engine. The purchase of the car left him with $19 in his bank account and an intense desire to enter it in the livestock show at the county fair. "What an oinker!" he says of the Chevrolet pony car.

Between 1975 and 1978, Jay began sculpting Sherlock Holmes characters. He had an agent in California who sold the sculptures in America and Europe. Unfortunately, the agent died. So did Jay's international sculpting career. However, he had done sculptures of the Beach Boys in 1975 and sent pictures to their manager. This brought him a big break, as the singing group's manager arranged for a meeting at CNE Stadium in Toronto, Canada.

"The sculptures wound up in the Brother Records recording studios in Santa Monica, California," Jay beams. "And Barbara and I wound up going on stage during the performance in Canada; the late Dennis Wilson, of the Beach Boys, turned out to be an exceptionally nice guy."

Three years later, Jay got another big break. It stemmed from an idea he got while recovering from a medical operation. Singers Jan and Dean were lip-synching the song "Dead Man's Curve" on television. Piersanti was inspired to do a sculpture. This eventually lead to the artist receiving a letter from Dean Torrence outlining arrangements for the two to meet in Washington, D.C. There, the young sculptor met the two members of the car/music fraternity of the 1960s at a club called The Cellar Door.

During a party following the Jan and Dean performance, the cartoonist was introduced to Ted Kennedy's personal secretary. This led to a commission for a sculpture depicting the politician at the wheel of his yacht. Piersanti later learned that the artwork became part of Kennedy's inner office decor.

Within a week of the Washington excitement in 1978, Jay placed a deposit on a "cherry" condition 1966 Corvette convertible that he purchased for $5,600. It had a numbers-matching 327-cubic-inch/300-horsepower V-8, four-speed gear box, factory side-pipes and removable hardtop.

The next day, Piersanti stumbled upon an even more original 1969 Corvette. Its 51,000 pampered miles were put on the odometer by an airline stewardess who flew more than she drove. Overcome by passion and devoid of reason, Jay also placed a deposit on this $5,100 car. "After three years of searching for the right Corvette, I bought two in two days," he remembers. "But my Dynaflow-destroying brother was still into cars, too. He bought the '66 and both cars have just been gems."

In 1982, Piersanti took his third shot at the "big time" by combining his car hobby with his artistic skills and creating cartoons for *Corvette Fever* magazine. Before too long, he got several assignments to illustrate articles and found his name listed in the magazine's staff credits. His association with *Corvette Fever* continues today.

Young Jeffrey Piersanti came into the world in 1983. "This almost took place in the front seat of my 1977 Malibu and I've always wondered if there was significance in that," says the proud father about the birth. "I think he takes after his mother, though; he didn't have any grease under his fingernails when he was born."

A book of Piersanti's Corvette cartoons called *My Corvette* was published in 1984. It was sold throughout the world via a distribution deal with Mike Yager of Mid-America Corvette. As a result, Jim Prather published some of Jay's cartoons in *Vette Vues* magazine. That same year, in the fall, Jay Piersanti created "Otto Mechanic" for *Old Cars*. He also picked up a 1964 Impala convertible in need of restoration. "Jeff was the only one-year-old on our block with his own ragtop," Piersanti believes. "It was an investment for the future for him."

The "Otto Mechanic" strip picked up its first "Moto" award from the National Automotive Journalism Association (NAJA) in 1986. It was presented during the NAJA conference at the Imperial Palace Hotel & Casino in Las Vegas, Nevada. The date was December 11. On December 7, 1988, the popular comic strip picked up its second motometer-shaped award from NAJA for "excellence in automotive journalism." As an offshoot of such honors, the automotive consultant, author, syndicated columnist and Society of Automotive Engineers member

Robert Sikorsky used an Otto cartoon in his 1990 book *Rip-Off Tip-Offs*.

In 1992, in the middle of a treacherous blizzard in western New York State, Piersanti attempted his first Otto painting. This delicate watercolor rendering became the color cover of the April 19, 1992 edition of *Old Cars*. In the fall of 1993, Piersanti was contacted about the compilation of this *Otto CAR-toons* book. Its publication seems a fitting honor for the comic strip's 10th year.

After a full decade and some 500 "Otto Mechanic" comic strips, the concepts and ideas keep popping up. "If this feature has brought *Old Cars* readers any joy during that time, it pales in comparison to the fun I've had drawing it," says Jay Piersanti. "With any luck, Otto and I will be around for another few decades or so."

Left: Dean Torrence (l.) of Jan and Dean met a young sculptor named Jay Piersanti in Washington, D.C. during 1978. Right: Piersanti today. In addition to cartooning, he is a teacher.

"Otto Mechanic"

By Jay Piersanti

"Otto Mechanic"

By Jay Piersanti

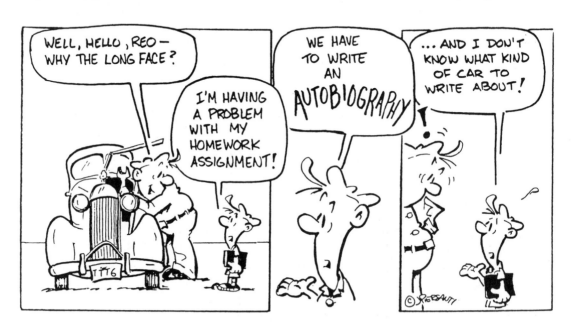

"Otto Mechanic"

By Jay Piersanti

"Otto Mechanic"

By Jay Piersanti

"Otto Mechanic"

By Jay Piersanti

"Otto Mechanic"

By Jay Piersanti

"Otto Mechanic"

By Jay Piersanti

"Otto Mechanic"

By Jay Piersanti

"Otto Mechanic"

By Jay Piersanti

"Otto Mechanic"

By Jay Piersanti

"Otto Mechanic"

By Jay Piersanti

"Otto Mechanic"

By Jay Piersanti

"Otto Mechanic"

By Jay Piersanti

"Otto Mechanic"

By Jay Piersanti

"Otto Mechanic"

By Jay Piersanti

"Otto Mechanic"

By Jay Piersanti

"Otto Mechanic"

By Jay Piersanti

"Otto Mechanic"

By Jay Piersanti

"Otto Mechanic"

By Jay Piersanti

"Otto Mechanic"

By Jay Piersanti

"Otto Mechanic"

By Jay Piersanti

"Otto Mechanic"

By Jay Piersanti

"Otto Mechanic"

By Jay Piersanti

"Otto Mechanic"

By Jay Piersanti

"Otto Mechanic"

By Jay Piersanti

"Otto Mechanic"

By Jay Piersanti

"Otto Mechanic"

By Jay Piersanti

"Otto Mechanic"

By Jay Piersanti

"Otto Mechanic"

By Jay Piersanti

"Otto Mechanic"

By Jay Piersanti

"Otto Mechanic"

By Jay Piersanti

"Otto Mechanic"

By Jay Piersanti

"Otto Mechanic"

By Jay Piersanti

"Otto Mechanic"

By Jay Piersanti

"Otto Mechanic"

By Jay Piersanti

"Otto Mechanic"

By Jay Piersanti

... AND WHEN THE FIRE-BREATHING, TWO-TON BEHEMOTH STALKED THE VILLAGE THE STREETS TREMBLED AND WINDOWS RATTLED!

UNTIL ONE DAY WHEN A HANDSOME YOUNG MAN ARRIVED WITH HIS TRUSTY PONY AND SLAUGHTERED THE HUGE BEAST RIGHT ON MAIN STREET!

AND THAT'S HOW I SHUT DOWN THE TRI-POWER BONNEVILLE WITH MY SHELBY MUSTANG!

"Otto Mechanic"

By Jay Piersanti

"Otto Mechanic"

By Jay Piersanti

"Otto Mechanic"

By Jay Piersanti

"Otto Mechanic"

By Jay Piersanti

"Otto Mechanic"

By Jay Piersanti

"Otto Mechanic"

By Jay Piersanti

"Otto Mechanic"

By Jay Piersanti

"Otto Mechanic"

By Jay Piersanti

"Otto Mechanic"

By Jay Piersanti

"Otto Mechanic"

By Jay Piersanti

"Otto Mechanic"

By Jay Piersanti

"Otto Mechanic"

By Jay Piersanti

"Otto Mechanic"

By Jay Piersanti

"Otto Mechanic"

By Jay Piersanti

"Otto Mechanic"

By Jay Piersanti

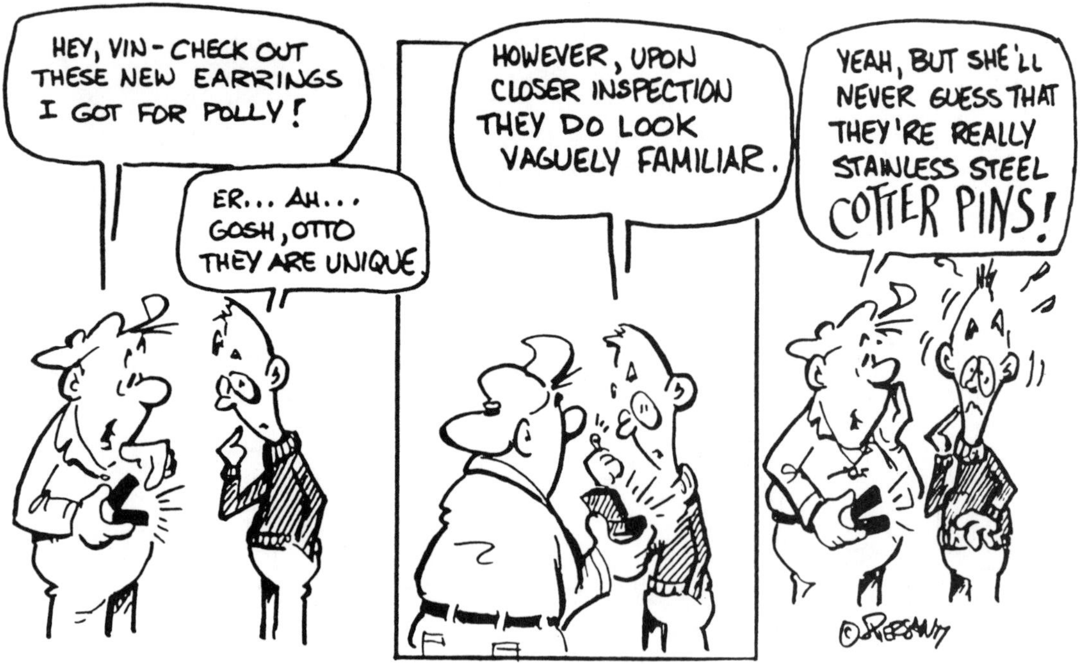

"Otto Mechanic"

By Jay Piersanti

"Otto Mechanic"

By Jay Piersanti

"Otto Mechanic"

By Jay Piersanti

"Otto Mechanic"

By Jay Piersanti

"Otto Mechanic"

By Jay Piersanti

"Otto Mechanic"

By Jay Piersanti

"Otto Mechanic"

By Jay Piersanti

"Otto Mechanic"

By Jay Piersanti

"Otto Mechanic"

By Jay Piersanti

"Otto Mechanic"

By Jay Piersanti

"Otto Mechanic"

By Jay Piersanti

"Otto Mechanic"

By Jay Piersanti

"Otto Mechanic"

By Jay Piersanti

"Otto Mechanic"

By Jay Piersanti

"Otto Mechanic"

By Jay Piersanti

"Otto Mechanic"

By Jay Piersanti

HELLO, OTTO — IT'S JUST ME, YOUR GIRLFRIEND, POLLY GLASS, WHO HASN'T HEARD FROM YOU IN OVER TWO WHOLE WEEKS!

I SUPPOSE YOU'VE BEEN TOO BUSY WITH YOUR CARS! WELL, I'VE HAD ENOUGH — WHICH WILL IT BE ... ME OR THE RUST BUCKETS? WELL? I'M WAITING...

JUST A SECOND — I'M LOOKING FOR A COIN TO FLIP.

"Otto Mechanic"

By Jay Piersanti

"Otto Mechanic"

By Jay Piersanti

"Otto Mechanic"

By Jay Piersanti

"Otto Mechanic"

By Jay Piersanti

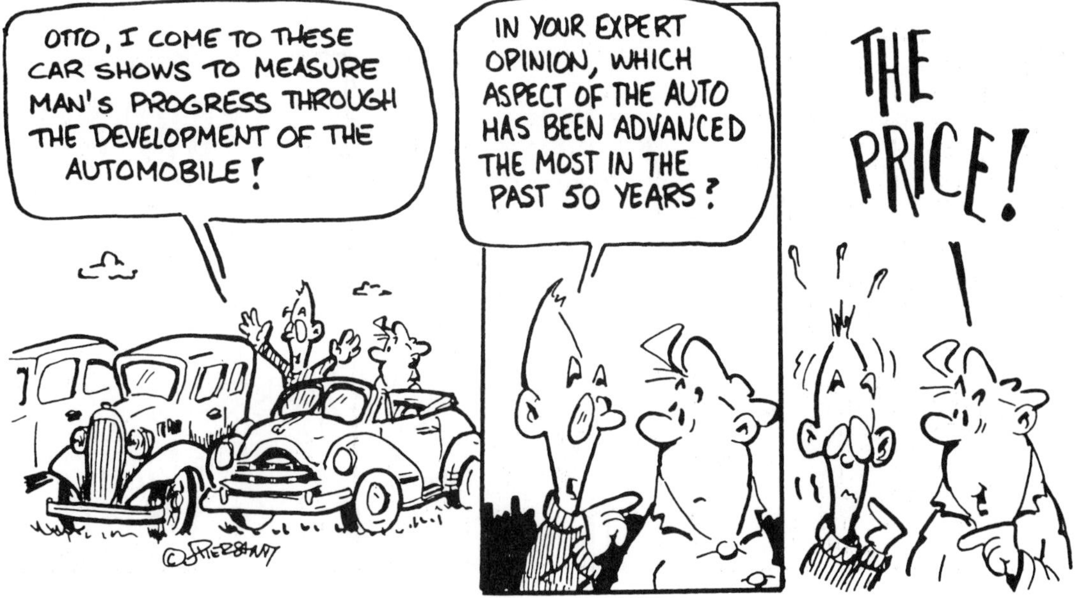

"Otto Mechanic"

By Jay Piersanti

"Otto Mechanic"

By Jay Piersanti

"Otto Mechanic"

By Jay Piersanti

"Otto Mechanic"

By Jay Piersanti

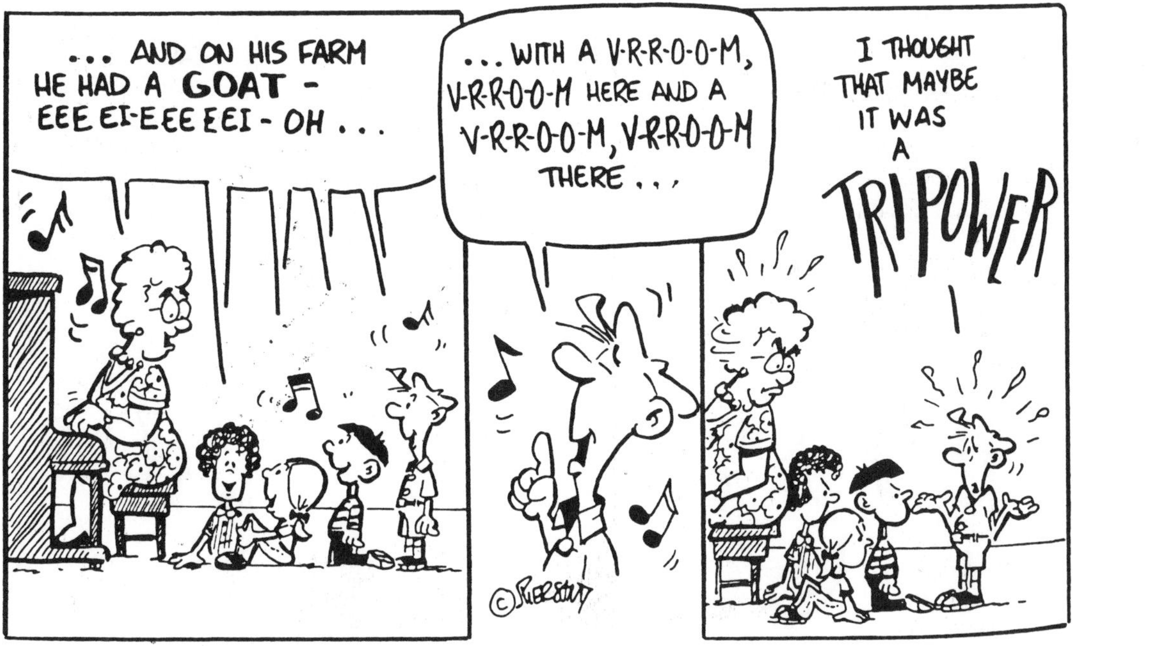

"Otto Mechanic"

By Jay Piersanti

"Otto Mechanic"

By Jay Piersanti

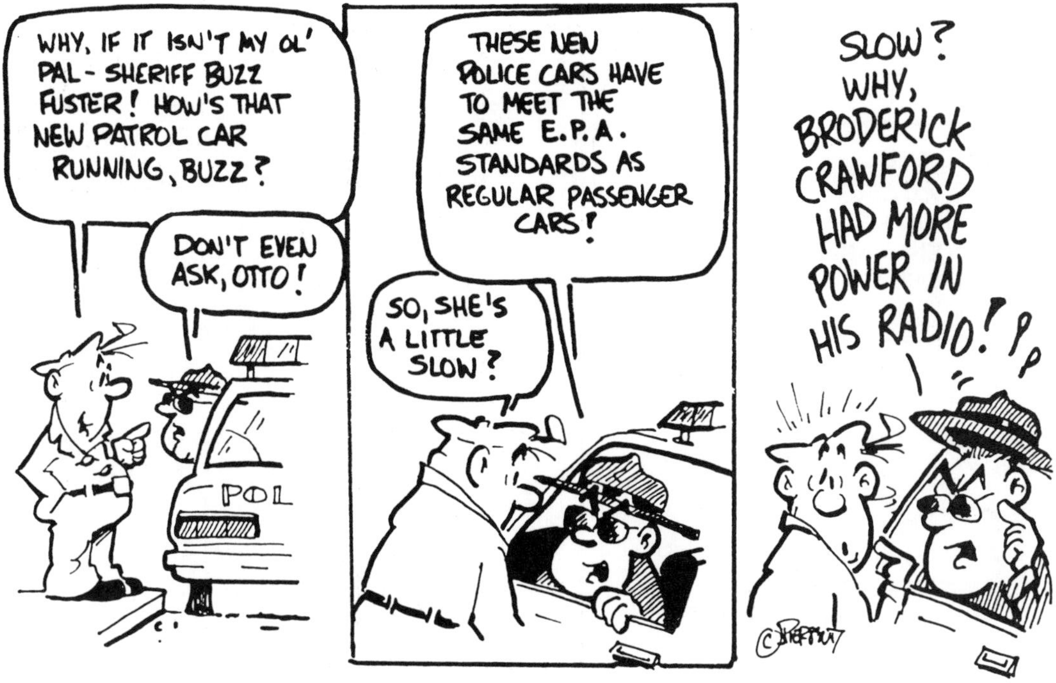

"Otto Mechanic"

By Jay Piersanti

"Otto Mechanic"

By Jay Piersanti